IMAGES
of America

BOSTON'S
BACK BAY

Members of the Boston Bicycle Club pose in front of Trinity Church in Copley Square in the late 1880s with their high-wheeled bicycles. The headquarters of the Boston Bicycle Club was located at 152 Newbury Street, designed by George F. Meacham, and built in 1884. Additions to the facade of Trinity Church included a porch and more elaborate roofs on the lanterns, completing Richardson's design. These bicycle enthusiasts look the epitome of sportsmen. (Courtesy of the Boston Public Library, hereinafter referred to as the BPL.)

On the cover: Boylston Street had become Boston's Fifth Avenue by the turn of the century, with churches, schools, and institutions lining the street from the Boston Common to the Back Bay Fens. These two residential hotels were typical of those built in the late nineteenth century. The Hotel Bristol, designed by L. Newcomb, was built at the corner of Boylston and Clarendon Streets in 1879. On the left is the Hotel Cluny, built in 1876 and designed by J.P. Putnam. (Courtesy of David Rooney.)

IMAGES
of America

BOSTON'S
BACK BAY

Anthony Mitchell Sammarco

ARCADIA

First published 1997
Copyright © Anthony Mitchell Sammarco, 1997

ISBN 0-7524-0828-3

Published by Arcadia Publishing,
an imprint of the Chalford Publishing Corporation,
One Washington Center, Dover, New Hampshire 03820.
Printed in Great Britain

Library of Congress Cataloging-in-Publication Data applied for

The townhouses of Dr. Henry W. Williams and William Moreland (15, 14, and 13 Arlington Street) were built in 1860 at the corner of Arlington and Newbury Streets, and were designed by the noted architect Richard Morris Hunt. Today, this is the site of the Ritz Carlton Hotel.

Contents

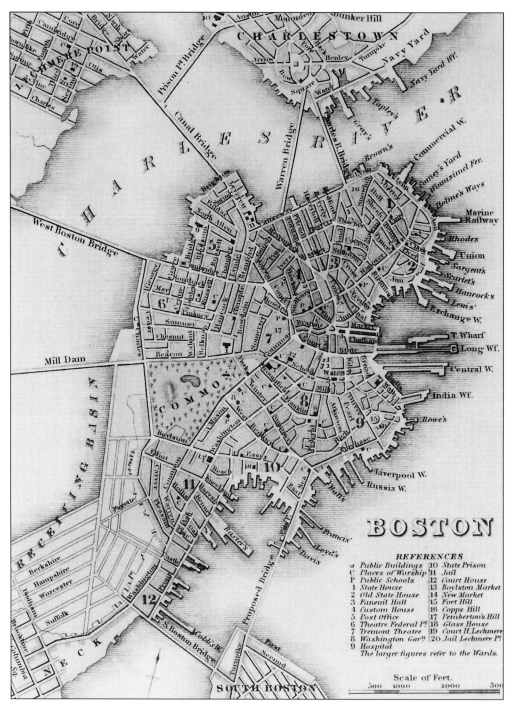

This 1833 map of Boston shows a densely built-up city, with bridges connecting Boston to Charlestown, Cambridge, Brookline, and South Boston. The new South End has been laid out on filled land and the Receiving Basin to the left of the Common would be the future site of the Back Bay of Boston.

Introduction

In the nineteenth century, the infilling of Boston's Back Bay was one of the greatest engineering feats in the world. The former marshlands and bay to the west of Boston Common stretched for a mile and a half to Muddy River, the present area of the Fenway, or the Back Bay Fens. Envisioned as a new section of the city that would combine both residential uses and a major square, the Back Bay was to become the quintessential Victorian neighborhood of nineteenth-century America.

On July 2, 1821, the Mill Dam was completed from the foot of Beacon Street at Charles Street across the Back Bay to Sewell's Point in Brookline, and was celebrated with great festivities and a cavalcade of citizens headed by William Hyslop Sumner, chief marshal of the event. The new road was a 50-foot wide, 1.5-mile toll road that saved one the effort of going to the mainland via Washington Street, the former "Neck" of Boston. The new Mill Dam, which was also to control the tidal flow from the Charles River into the Back Bay and provide waterpower for some of the industries located in the area of Gravelly Point, was initially known as Western Avenue but was later named Beacon Street. This development began the westward glance of Bostonians towards an area that might eventually be developed. As early as the first decade of the nineteenth century, Bostonians had begun cutting down the hills and using the soil to fill in the marshland; Beacon Hill, which once rose to the height of the dome of the Massachusetts State House, was cut down and carted to the foot of the hill and used to create Charles Street (the "flat" of Beacon Hill). This same technique was used when the area bound by Charles, Boylston, Beacon, and Arlington Streets was infilled with trash, refuse, and any other solid landfill available for the anticipated Public Garden, which was opened to the public in 1837.

The lack of tidal flow in the Back Bay became a problem as early as 1814, when the Mill Dam was begun. It caused noxious odors and stagnation in the marshlands to increase. By the mid-1830s, roadbeds for the railroads had been built to allow the Boston and Providence and the Boston and Worcester Railroads to pass through the Back Bay. The marshes had uneven depth, and it was thought that infill of the area would preclude an end to the pervasive odors—which had ultimately come to the attention of the Boston Board of Health—and also provide over 500 acres of land that could be filled and developed. The project was a daunting one. The Commonwealth of Massachusetts allowed the infilling process to begin in the late 1850s, and so began the greatest change in Boston's topographical history.

The massive project was assigned by the Commonwealth of Massachusetts to the Boston engineering firm of Goss and Munson, and the stupendous task fell on the shoulders of John Souther (1816-1911), a South Boston resident who invented the steam-powered "Souther Steamshovel." A successful engineer who worked at the Globe Locomotive Works in South Boston, Souther began dredging the marshes of the Back Bay and preparing a railroad line that connected Needham to the project site. Souther's steam shovel literally "strip-mined" the hills of Needham in the area of Highland and Gould Streets to provide a sufficient amount of fill. For over three decades, the soil, sand, and rock fill was sent the 9 miles to Boston's Back Bay by open gondola cars every forty-five minutes, twenty-four hours a day, six days a week. Once these gondola cars arrived at the site of the area being filled, they would be tipped on a spring and their loads would be dumped into the marshes. The area from the Public Garden to the Muddy River, the area now known as the Fenway of Boston, was eventually filled with earth from Needham via this laborious procedure.

The laying out of the streets in the new "West End" of Boston, as the new area was initially referred to, fell to Arthur Gilman, a well-known architect who had designed the Arlington Street Church, the first church to move from downtown Boston (the former Federal Street Church). Gilman created a grid plan of wide avenues, two of which perpetuated the eighteenth-century names of portions of Washington Street—Marlborough and Newbury Streets. Commonwealth Avenue, a 200-foot-wide avenue with a central park extending its length from the Public Garden to Massachusetts Avenue, was the grandest of the streets and was planted with a four-wide row alley of trees. The cross streets, running from north to south, were named after British earldoms and included Arlington, Berkeley, Clarendon, Dartmouth, Exeter, Fairfield, Gloucester, and Hereford Streets. The correlation of the wide streets of the Back Bay to Parisian boulevards was obvious, but the long-nurtured ties between Boston and Britain were obvious in the names selected. The new Back Bay, built on filled land with hundreds of thousands of pilings driven deep into the earth, supported monumental churches, educational buildings, and townhouses. The neighborhood came to represent the height of respectability, with families purchasing building lots at auction and deciding upon an architect to design their "in-town" house. From 1860, when the first townhouses were completed on Beacon Street between Arlington and Berkeley Streets, the wide array of architectural styles of the houses of the Back Bay would create one of the most cohesive and well-planned residential districts in this country, and in turn the epitome of a Brahmin residential enclave of the nineteenth century.

Today, few of the townhouses are used as single-family homes, for they have proven far too cumbersome and large for this function. However, the Back Bay plan has survived—remarkably intact and the neighborhood now known as the Back Bay Historic District boasts impressive streetscapes of brownstone, brick, and limestone townhouses. The Back Bay Architectural Commission was established in 1966 to oversee any exterior changes to structures in this historic area.

In particular, one townhouse survives unaltered today and poignantly offers a glimpse into how a Back Bay family lived in the mid- and late nineteenth century. The Gibson House Museum at 137 Beacon Street, between Arlington and Berkeley Streets, was designed by Edward Clarke Cabot for the Gibson Family, whose fortune was derived from the Cuban sugar trade. Occupied by three generations of the family from the time it was completed in 1860 until 1954 when Charles Hammond Gibson Jr. died, this house museum is the historic house of Boston's Back Bay. As Christopher Lydon, a thoughtful observer, once remarked, "The Gibson House seems as if it is preserved in amber."

One
The Public Garden

The lagoon of the Public Garden offers a tranquil spot in a busy area of Boston's Back Bay. In this c. 1900 photograph, an awning-festooned swan boat nears the suspension bridge designed by William Gibbons Preston (it is ironically the smallest true suspension bridge in the world). The serpentine path in the foreground followed the irregular contours of the lagoon, and offers a pleasant place to stroll on a warm summer afternoon.

In this 1860 photograph that looks from the corner of Charles and Beacon Streets, the Public Garden can be seen just past the trees. The area west of Arlington Street has not yet been infilled and would shortly be known as the new "West End," or the Back Bay of Boston. The Public Garden was the brainchild of Horace Gray, who based his idea on European models; the first proprietors of the Botanic Garden in Boston were Horace Gray, Charles Curtis, and George Darracott.

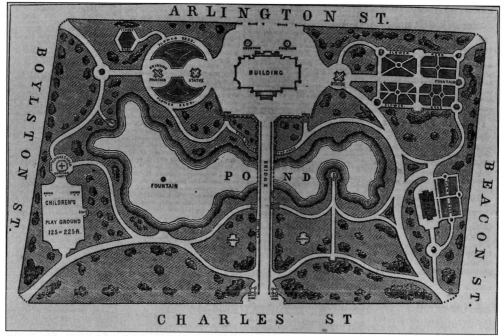

George Meacham's plan for the Public Garden included a central pond, often referred to as the lagoon, formal flowerbeds, and serpentine paths that surrounded an open, tree-studded park of 24.25 acres in the middle of the city. Bounded on all four sides by Arlington, Beacon, Charles, and Beacon Streets, it was filled with statuary, fountains, and monuments; it also contained a large glass conservatory near Charles Street.

A Bird's Eye View of Boston and Its Surroundings in 1850 is the title of a superb lithograph by J. Bachman that looks towards the Public Garden and the Common with Boston just beyond. On the left is the Mill Dam, present-day Beacon Street, and an alley of trees lining Arlington Street, which is the boundary for the marshlands of the Back Bay.

Horace Gray was a noted horticulturist who envisioned a botanical garden on the newly filled lands west of Charles Street. In 1837, the Public Garden was laid out and planted with flowerbeds for the enjoyment of the public.

Ralph Waldo Emerson and Oliver Wendell Holmes sit on a bench conversing near the glass conservatory in the Public Garden along Charles Street in 1857. In the early years, many of the beds were experimental, with flowers being set out in the spring. Notice how young many of the trees on the right are.

This Victorian couple has paused in their perambulation around the Public Garden to admire one of the playing fountains near the glass conservatory, where camellias bloomed during the long winter months.

A young boy walks along the serpentine path that encircles the lagoon as canoeists paddle in the pond. Notice the wrought-iron summerhouse on the Lilliputian center island.

By 1875, although the Public Garden was laid out with lawns and bedded-out displays, the trees were still young and would not offer copious amounts of shade for a few more years. Though designed by George F. Meacham, the flowerbeds and pathways were laid out by John Galvin, then city forester.

The suspension bridge that spans the lagoon is the shortest true suspension bridge in the world. Designed by architect William Gibbons Preston (1842–1910) and civil engineer Clemens Herschel (1842–1930) and built in 1867, it is as attractive an addition to the Public Garden as it is useful. Notice 12 Arlington Street, the Bates-Sears House, which is at the corner of Arlington Street and Commonwealth Avenue.

Looking from the suspension bridge toward the equestrian statue of General George Washington, huge pots planted with succulents may be seen in this photograph from 1880. Notice the Commonwealth Avenue Mall and the uniformity of the rooflines of the townhouses. One of the basic premises of the Back Bay was that individual townhouses created a streetscape, achieving a total effect rather than a singular one.

A statue of Venus rising from an oyster shell was in the center of one of the circular pools beside the equestrian statue of General Washington. Often referred to as "Venus on the Half Shell" or the "Maid of the Mist," this was one of numerous statues set out in the Public Garden in the nineteenth century.

A family admires the equestrian statue of Washington that was sculpted by Thomas Ball (1819–1911) in Rome and erected in the Public Garden in 1869 at a cost of $42,000. The townhouses in the distance were built on Beacon Street, the former Mill Dam, between 1848 and 1852.

The Ether Monument was designed by John Quincy Adams Ward and was donated by Thomas Lee. Dedicated in 1868, the monument was erected "as an expression of gratitude for the relief of human suffering occasioned by the discovery of the anaesthetic properties of sulphuric ether." Commemorating the first use of ether in an operation by Dr. William T.G. Morton at the Massachusetts General Hospital in 1847, the statue "proved to the world that inhaling of ether causes insensibility to pain."

A panoramic view of the Public Garden about 1890 from the spire of the Arlington Street Church shows the mature plantings and trees that offered respite during the summer months. The flat of Beacon Hill can be seen on the left with the spire of the Church of the Advent; the dome of the Massachusetts State House can be seen on the far right.

Members of the Roxbury City Guard pose in the Public Garden on September 13, 1870, in front of Thomas Ball's equestrian statue of George Washington. The townhouses in the background were built on Beacon Street, the former Mill Dam, and those on the left were built on Arlington Street after 1859, when the infilling of the Back Bay was commenced. (Courtesy of The Boston Athenaeum.)

The swan boats were introduced to the Public Garden by Robert Paget in 1877. The graceful gliding swans, which are still furiously peddled by employees of the Pagets, were inspired by the opera Lohengren. The spire of the Arlington Street Church rises in the distance; Boylston Street was once a solid block. Arlington Street was not cut through until 1902 when 110, 111, and 112 Boylston Street were demolished just four decades after they were built.

The striped canvas awnings on the swan boats added a festive air to the Public Garden as well as protection from the sun, as seen in this photograph of 1880. On the right can be seen the tower of the Park Square Depot of the Boston and Providence Railroad. Designed by Peabody and Stearns and built in 1872, it was later demolished and the Hotel Statler, now the Park Plaza Hotel, was built on its site.

A swan boat gracefully glides toward the suspension bridge as people line the railings.

The lagoon had been planted with weeping willows that gracefully arched over the edge of the pond. During the winter, the pond was flooded and allowed to freeze and was swiftly "covered by a gay throng of happy youth, whose skates glisten in the sun and whose merry voices ring out joyously on the air." This photograph looks from the area near the corner of Boylston and Arlington Streets.

By the early 1930s, the swan boats had become synonymous with the Public Garden. School children flocked to the lagoon in June for the long-anticipated annual swan boat ride. Tourist and native alike still delight in taking a graceful and relaxing trip around the pond while tossing peanuts to the ducks and swans.

The plantings in the Public Garden created a great maintenance chore, but the effects were well worth the effort. The flowerbeds lining the walkways burst forth with color three seasons of the year, and provided much enjoyment for those strolling through the garden or simply cutting through to get from one side of town to the other.

William Doogue was appointed superintendent of the Public Garden in 1878 and was said to be "ever willing to impart information to citizens and the many strangers who visit the Garden during the summer." His floral displays of army, navy, Grand Army, and other badges in the Public Garden on the occasion of the meeting of the Grand Army of the Republic in Boston in 1890 brought him many compliments.

20

One of the ponds had a statue titled *Venus at the Bath* in the center with water spraying up around it. This marble statue was given by Joshua D. Bates, philanthropist and patron of the Boston Public Library, and was the first work of art to be placed in the Public Garden. In the distance is the townhouse of Bayard Thayer, designed by Ogden Codman and built in 1911; today, the Thayer House is the Hampshire House, the inspiration for the bar setting of the ever-popular sitcom Cheers.

In this photograph of the Public Garden about 1875, the pathways were dotted with circular ponds and monuments, with trees having been planted in great profusion. The first monument to be erected in the Public Garden was the bronze statue of Edward Everett, modeled by William W. Story; this statue is now at Edward Everett Square, opposite Everett's birthplace in Dorchester.

Park workers are planting tulip bulbs in a flowerbed in the Public Garden in this photograph of 1903. Tulips were once such a rare flower that the first tulip bed in America was planted in the Public Garden. Notice how the bed has been prepared, with each worker planting the bulbs in a strategic spot. It was said of these displays that the numbers of tulip bulbs used was "well-nigh incredible."

Two men stroll along a path near the equestrian statue of General George Washington (1732–1799). Notice the lavish plantings in the beds on either side of the pathway, including giant palm trees that were set out in the spring after having spent the winter in the city's glass conservatories.

Looking west in the Public Garden, the center pathway leading to the gates opposite the Commonwealth Avenue Mall, the lavish flowerbeds, and carpet-like lawns have created welcome respite from summer heat since the Public Garden was opened to Bostonians in 1837.

The Public Garden even has charm in the winter. Generations of Boston's youth have eagerly awaited the freezing-over of the lagoon for ice-skating and enjoyed playing on the snow-covered lawns and frozen pond.

One of the newest pieces of art to be placed in the Public Garden is the Mallard Family, a set of eight bronze ducklings and a mother duck that was presented in 1987 by the Friends of the Public Garden. In Robert McCloskey's perennial classic, *Make Way For Ducklings*, Mrs. Mallard leads her brood—Jack, Kack, Lack, Mack, Nack, Ouack, Pack, and Quack—from the Charles River down Mount Vernon Street to their eventual home in the Public Garden.

The George Robert White monument was designed by Daniel Chester French and placed in the corner of the Public Garden at the junction of Beacon and Arlington Streets. George R. White (1847–1922) was a philanthropist and public benefactor whose legacy survives to this day. The monument is inscribed: "Cast Thy Bread Upon The Waters For Thou Shalt Find It After Many Days."

Two

The Beginnings of the Back Bay

The print *A Bird's Eye View of Boston and Its Surroundings* was done in 1850 and showed the Public Garden with a tree-lined Arlington Street as the edge of the Back Bay. On the left are townhouses along the Mill Dam, present-day Beacon Street, that were built in the 1850s.

A man purchases an apple from the "Apple Lady," who seemed to be a perennial fixture at the corner of the Boston Common at Boylston and Charles Streets in the mid-nineteenth century. In the distance can be seen the second edifice of the Boston and Providence Railroad Depot at Park Square; on the far left is the former townhouse of Winslow Lewis, which was built c. 1820 and demolished in 1870.

Looking toward Park Square in 1840 from the intersection of the Providence and Worcester Railroads, three pedestrians travel along a filled train embankment as a train passes them headed into Boston. The marshland of the Back Bay is evident on either side of the railroad beds and might have had the depth of a few inches or a few feet.

Looking west through the granite gateposts on the Boston Common at the corner of Boylston and Charles Streets, the south side of Boylston Street was lined with brick townhouses built between 1848 and 1850 that faced the Public Garden. On the right can be seen the spire of the Arlington Street Church, designed by Arthur Gilman and Gridley J. Fox Bryant and completed in 1860.

The Park Square station of the New York, New Haven and Hartford Railroad, seen here in 1895, was designed by the architectural firm of Peabody and Stearns and built in 1872. The depot had reading, dining, billiard, and smoking rooms as well as a barbershop and washrooms. On the left is the statue of Abraham Lincoln known as the Emancipation Group Monument by Thomas Ball. The base of the monument reads:

*A Rage Set Free
And The Country At Peace
LINCOLN
Rests From His Labors.*

The Public Garden, seen here in 1857, was bordered by Beacon and Charles Streets. The area to the left was to undergo tremendous topographical changes within the next few years through the massive infill project.

Looking west from the dome of the Massachusetts State House in 1857, Beacon Street (the former Mill Dam) extends from the corner of Charles Street to Brookline at the Punch Bowl. What would become the Back Bay is the marshland to the left. The area was infilled over the next three decades to create a quintessential Victorian neighborhood of nineteenth-century America.

Looking toward Boston from the eastern slope of Parker Hill in Roxbury in 1828, the marshes of the Back Bay lie between Beacon Hill and Roxbury. The dome of the Massachusetts State House caps Beacon Hill and the densely built houses descend the western slope of Beacon Hill toward what would be infilled for the new lands.

John Souther stands in front of the steam shovel that would dredge the hills of Needham for gravel to be used in the infilling of the marshes of the Back Bay. The gondola train in the background would travel for nearly four decades between Needham and the Back Bay twenty-four hours a day, six days a week before the project was completed. (Courtesy of The Boston Athenaeum.)

John Souther was a native of South Boston and an engineer with the Hinckley Locomotive Works before he established the first locomotive works in South Boston in the 1840s. During the next five decades, he produced "a variety of machinery for carrying out the greatest national enterprises and public improvements of the nineteenth century."

A diorama of the infilling of the Back Bay was exhibited at the New England Mutual Life Insurance Company (now The New England) for many years. The train, consisting of thirty-five gondola cars bearing gravel, can be seen on the right with the tip cart dumping its load of fill into the marshes. The gravel train made twenty-five trips per day, moving 2,500 cubic yards of fill daily from Needham to the Back Bay. (Courtesy of *The New England*.)

Winslow Homer sketched some of the determined scavengers who arrived en masse in the Back Bay for *Ballou's Pictoral Drawing Room Companion* on May 21, 1858. The fill was dumped from tip carts that stopped on the Mill Dam, and included everything from ashes and street sweepings to empty bottles, broken furniture, and refuse. The often-quoted saying "one man's trash is another man's gold" was never more true than in this case!

The Souther steam shovel was an engineering miracle that was able to load gondola cars with enough fill to complete two house lots per day. Numerous spectators traveled to Needham—only 9 miles away from the Back Bay—to watch the operation.

Looking toward Arlington Street from a fountain in the Public Garden, the townhouse of John Bates, later that of J. Mongomery Sears, can be seen in the center at the corner of Commonwealth Avenue.

Looking from the tower of the Park Square Terminus, the Public Garden was embellished with trees and statuary by the 1880s, making it not only an enjoyable place to visit, but an ornament within the city. On the left is Arlington Street in the new Back Bay and on the far right are the townhouses built prior to the Civil War on the flat of Beacon Hill. (Courtesy of David Rooney.)

The Arlington Street Church was the first religious congregation to relocate to the Back Bay. Built in 1860 and designed by Arthur Gilman and Gridley J. Fox Bryant, the former Federal Street Church was rebuilt at the corner of Arlington and Boylston Streets. On the left is Boylston Street, which contained a solid row of townhouses until 1902 when Arlington Street was extended to Tremont Street.

Looking toward the Public Garden from the spire of the Arlington Street Church in 1890, the site of the former ropewalks had been transformed into a 25-acre park. The spires belong to, from the left, the Park Square Depot, the Arlington Street Church, Trinity Church, and the Central Congregational Church (now the Church of the Covenant).

Looking down Arlington Street from Boylston Street in 1900, one might think he was in either Paris or London, given the wide boulevard lined with French mansard-roofed townhouses facing the Public Garden. Arlington Street was laid out in 1858 as a 60-foot-wide street lighted by gas lamps; the Back Bay was the epitome of cosmopolitan living.

The Arlington Street Church was to have townhouses built on either side of it by 1872; on the right are the townhouses of the Bates, Clark, Conant, and Preston Families and to the left is that of Dr. George Lyman. A corner of the Public Garden can be seen on the right, and in the distance at the corner of Boylston and Berkeley Streets can be seen the natural history museum (now Louis of Boston). (Courtesy of The Boston Athenaeum.)

Three
The Early Back Bay

Looking west from the dome of the Massachusetts State House in the early 1870s, the Back Bay had been extended as far as Clarendon Street. The spires of the Arlington Street Church, on the left, and the Central Congregational Church (now the Church of the Covenant) rise above the new townhouses. (Courtesy of The Boston Athenaeum.)

About 1870, Arlington Street was an impressive thoroughfare lined with equally impressive townhouses creating a uniform streetscape that faced the lush green space of the Public Garden. (Courtesy of The Boston Athenaeum.)

Sitting in his "Victoria" carriage is Nathan Appleton in front of the duplex townhouse of Erastus Bigelow and Thomas Gold Appleton at 8 and 10 Commonwealth Avenue. Built in 1864 as French Academic style townhouses, the two structures were demolished in the late 1950s and are now the site of Carlton House.

Thomas Gold Appleton (1812–1884) was a poet and essayist and a great wit whose bon mots included a reference to Nahant, a popular nineteenth-century summer resort for Bostonians, as "cold roast Boston." Ralph Waldo Emerson called Appleton the first conversationalist in America.

This photograph looks west on the Commonwealth Avenue Mall from the Public Garden about 1870. The north side of the mall extended to Clarendon Street by this time.

About 1870, the south side of the Commonwealth Avenue Mall was more uniform in its height and facades than the north side.

A horse-drawn sleigh passes the Commonwealth Avenue Mall at Berkeley Street about 1885. In the distance can be seen the spire of the Brattle Square Church, now the First Baptist Church in Boston.

This 1876 image of the intersection of Commonwealth Avenue and Dartmouth Street illustrates the fact that townhouses were not built one after the other, but as owners built houses or developed their land for speculative purposes. Streets were filled to the level of the Mill Dam, 17 feet above low tide, but the building lots were 5 feet lower, precluding a basement. In the center is the Ames-Webster House, now the architectural office of Childs Bertman Tseckares Casendino. (Courtesy of The Boston Athenaeum.)

Looking east on Commonwealth Avenue at the turn of the century, the trees lining the mall appear as mature shade trees and the townhouses create a uniformity from Arlington Street to Massachusetts Avenue. On the right is the spire of the Brattle Square Church, now the First Baptist Church, and on the left is the spire of the Church of the Advent on Brimmer Street. (Courtesy of The Boston Athenaeum.)

A statue of Alexander Hamilton (1757–1804) by William Rimmer has graced the Commonwealth Avenue Mall near Arlington Street since 1865. Orator, writer, soldier, and jurist, Hamilton was the United States secretary of the treasury when he was killed in a duel with Aaron Burr. Hamilton's likeness is well known to all, as it appears on every ten-dollar bill!

The Hotel Vendome is in the center of this 1892 photograph with townhouses and churches of the Back Bay on either side. The churches are, from the left, Brattle Square (now the First Baptist Church), Central Congregational (now the Church of the Covenant), Arlington Street Church, and Trinity Church.

A seated statue of the great abolitionist William Lloyd Garrison (1805–1897), sculpted in 1886 by Olin Levi Warner, graces the Commonwealth Avenue Mall opposite the Hotel Vendome. Publisher of *The Liberator*, Garrison's views of slavery were as vociferous as they were sincere and Garrison's first editorial contained these words, which are carved on the statue's base: "I am in earnest—I will not equivocate—I will not retreat a single inch—and I will be heard."

The Russell and Gibson Houses were built in 1859 at 135 and 137 Beacon Street, the former Mill Dam, and were designed by Edward Clarke Cabot as brick and brownstone Italian Renaissance Revival townhouses for relatives Samuel Hammond Russell and Catherine Hammond Gibson, widow of John Gardiner Gibson. The Gibson House became a museum in 1957 and is today the only house museum in the Back Bay. (Courtesy of The Gibson House Museum.)

Charles Hammond Gibson Jr. (1874–1954) was a bon vivant, poet, and author who lived at 137 Beacon Street. The following sonnet, *Remember Me*, was published in *The Spur* in 1938:

Oh, I would have you once rember me,
Not as I am, with suffering that mars
The countenance, and seared with countless scars,
But as I was, a youth of twenty three,
Fresh-fashioned for the life that was to be,
Full of those winged flights among the stars,
We would adventure to, ere fortune bars
The way. Good friend, I think you must agree,
That in Times' journey onwards, we attain
To greater heights and depths, o'er land and sea
Yet ever must those halycon days remain,
Loving and loved, for what we could not see
Was nature's gift, that life so soon can stain.
So, in youth's glorious hours remember me!

(Courtesy of The Gibson House Museum.)

John Marquand interviewed Charles Hammond Gibson for his article on Boston that appeared in the March 24, 1941 edition of *Life* magazine. Gibson sits at his desk with a portrait of his grandmother, Catherine Hammond Gibson, on the right and a double portrait of his sisters Mary Ethel (Mrs. Freeman Allen) and Rosamond (Mrs. Warren Winslow) on the left. Marquand sits in a Sleepy Hollow chaise lounge in a remarkably intact Victorian library interior. (Courtesy of The Gibson House Museum.)

The Victorian Society decorates The Gibson House for its annual Victorian Holiday Open House (the first Monday in December), which attracts numerous and supporters who revel en costume. The re-enactors at the 1996 event were (first row) Katy Bishop, Helen Hannon, Lorah Snow, Sally Mummey, and Debbie Franco-Andrade; (second row) Cynthia Snow, Barbara Pugliese, Jan Turnquist, Sue Lomauro, and Megan Hill; (third row) Dan Downing, Brian Powell, Bill Harrington, Ben Bishop, Steve Eames, Steve Hill, Steve Bilyea, and Joseph Coletti. (Photograph by Steve Gyurina, courtesy of The Victorian Society.)

A panorama of the Back Bay in 1895 from the dome of the Massachusetts State House shows an elegant residential neighborhood built on filled land. Beacon Street, on the right, was the former Mill Dam and was lined with impressive townhouses.

Looking west on Newbury Street from the Public Garden about 1875, the spire of the Central Congregational Church (now the Church of the Covenant) breaks the uniformity of the rooflines of the townhouses.

Newbury Street was named after the renaming of a portion of what is now Washington Street in 1824 in honor of General George Washington. The new street was to run from Arlington Street to Massachusetts Avenue and was a residential street until the early twentieth century. In this photograph, Emmanuel Church is on the right and the spire of the Central Congregational Church (now the Church of the Covenant) rises on the left. (Courtesy of David Rooney.)

Looking toward the Massachusetts State House from the tower of the New Old South Church in Copley Square about 1880, Newbury Street appears in the foreground. The vacant lots between Clarendon and Dartmouth Streets would shortly contain townhouses to complete the streetscape.

Looking east on Newbury Street from Clarendon Street about 1900, we see the Walker Building and the Rogers Building of the Massachusetts Institute of Technology on the right, townhouses along Newbury Street, and the spire of the Central Congregational Church (now the Church of the Covenant) in the center.

The Back Bay was serviced by a horse car that operated on Marlborough Street and Commonwealth Avenue and provided access to the Public Garden and the Art Museum in Copley Square. This was horse car #451, photographed at the Bartlett Street Carbarn in Roxbury. (Courtesy of David Rooney.)

A horse car stops on Marlborough Street to allow passengers to enter. This horse-drawn car was to serve the Back Bay until December 24, 1899, when the line was retired from service. (Courtesy of David Rooney.)

The townhouse of Oliver Wendell Holmes was built in 1870 at 296 Beacon Street, on the water side of Beacon Street, one of the city's more prestigious addresses. An unpretentious and unassuming house, it was nonetheless on the correct side of the street! The Holmes family lived here until an apartment building was built on the site in 1951; their residence spanned a remarkably long period of time in the context of the Back Bay.

Dr. Oliver Wendell Holmes (1809–1894) was photographed in 1888 in his library at his Back Bay townhouse. Holmes had acquired 294 Beacon Street as a library extension to his townhouse, a necessity due to the large library he acquired after his career as professor of anatomy at the Harvard Medical School.

Looking north from the roof of the First Unitarian Church at the corner of Berkeley and Marlborough Streets about 1885, the uniformity of the rooflines never has seemed more apparent. The Charles River is just beyond the townhouses and the Charles River Bridge, connecting Boston and Cambridge, is seen in the distance.

The townhouse of the Webster family was designed by John Hubbard Sturgis and built in 1872 at 306 Dartmouth Street as a very French mansion with a mansard roof and a conservatory on the left. (Courtesy of The Boston Athenaeum.)

The Cushing-Endicott House was designed by Snell and Gregerson and built in 1871 at the corner of Dartmouth and Marlborough Streets for Thomas Cushing, a China trade merchant. (Courtesy of The Boston Athenaeum.)

The rectory for Trinity Church was designed by H.H. Richardson and built in 1879 at the corner of Clarendon and Newbury Streets. An impressive design with a massive Romanesque arch leading to the entrance, the rectory would later be enlarged with a third floor. On the right is the spire of the Central Congregational Church, now the Church of the Covenant.

Peabody and Stearns designed this townhouse between 1877 and 1879 for John C. Phillips at 299 Berkeley Street on the corner of Marlborough Street. This is now the site of the First Lutheran Church of Boston, designed by Pietro Belluschi and built in 1959.

Designed by Kirby and Lewis for speculator Asa Caton, 323 Commonwealth Avenue was purchased by Horace Billings and 321 Commonwealth Avenue was purchased by H. Tuttle. The cast-iron fence in the foreground lined the Commonwealth Avenue Mall.

Kirby and Lewis designed these townhouses along Commonwealth Avenue. Notice the vacant lots on either side of the townhouses and the uncompleted townhouses on the next block, seen on the far right.

Cabot and Chandler designed this townhouse in 1880 as a Queen Anne extravaganza with cut-brick details and a dramatic sunburst above the second-floor window. Built at 135 Marlborough Street for Henry Lee, its red brick was more English in feeling than the earlier French Academic style of the Back Bay.

Two townhouses at 176 and 178 Commonwealth Avenue were designed by Charles Atwood and were built of brownstone with fanciful dormers projecting from conically shaped turrets. The townhouses adjoin a classically inspired apartment building designed by G.N. Jacobs at 182 Commonwealth Avenue. (Courtesy of David Rooney.)

The John Andrew House was designed by the architectural firm of McKim, Mead and White and was built in 1884 at the corner of Commonwealth Avenue and Gloucester Street. A balcony on the third floor facade was brought from the Tuilleries in Paris. (Courtesy of John B. Fox.)

Rotch and Tilden designed this townhouse in 1892 for Herbert Sears at 287 Commonwealth Avenue. A grand mansion with a Greek portico surmounted by an anthemion crest, the interior was redesigned by Ogden Codman in 1904. For the last few decades, this has been the headquarters of the International Institute of Boston, which was founded in 1924 to assist immigrants and refugees. (Courtesy of The Boston Athenaeum.)

The wide range of architectural styles being utilized in the Back Bay at the turn of the century is evident in these three townhouses. From the left are 474 Commonwealth Avenue (built 1900 and designed by S.D. Kelly), 476 Commonwealth Avenue (built 1900 and designed by W. Whitney Lewis), and 478 Commonwealth Avenue (built 1903 and designed by Kilham and Hopkins). (Courtesy of David Rooney.)

The Albert Burrage Mansion was designed by Charles E. Brigham and built in 1899 at 314 Commonwealth Avenue. One of the grandest townhouses in the Back Bay and "one of the most imposing of any residence which its architect has designed," it was a less ostentatious version of the chateaux being built in New York. The Boston Evening Clinic was located here for many years, and today the structure serves as Burrage House, a luxury retirement home.

Alvan T. Fuller (1878–1958) operated a Packard automobile dealership on Commonwealth Avenue, but also served as a member of Congress and governor of Massachusetts from 1925 to 1929. His townhouse at 150 Beacon Street was designed by Alexander Wadsworth Longfellow and was built in 1904 on the site of John Lowell and Isabella Stewart Gardner's townhouse.

Although the townhouse at 150 Beacon Street was built on the site of the Gardner's townhouse in 1904, it did not share the same street number as the former residence. Isabella Stewart Gardner stipulated that "152" was to be retired when Fenway Court was built. The elegant facade of this townhouse, originally built for E.S. Draper, was a classically inspired design with an impressive roof balustrade.

This view of the Commonwealth Avenue Mall, looking east, shows the impressive grandeur of this boulevard. Infilled between 1859 and the mid-1880s when it reached Massachusetts Avenue, this tree-lined park had impressive townhouses of varied designs built on either side.

United States troops march down Beacon Street after mobilization in October 1894 during the Spanish-American War. Notice the varied architectural styles of the townhouses on the right.

The junction of Commonwealth and Massachusetts Avenues was home to a combination of townhouses and residential apartment buildings. On the left is an apartment building at 371 Commonwealth Avenue that was designed by McKay and Dunham and built in 1892. The townhouse on the opposite corner was that of Governor Oliver Ames, designed by Carl Fehmer and built in 1882.

A new map of Boston comprising the whole city with new boundaries of the ward was engraved for the 1859 edition of the Boston Almanac. Boston had been substantially increased topographically by the infilling of the South End (left center) and the implementation of the grid plan for the new Back Bay. The population of Boston by 1860 had reached 177,840 people, and through the creation of new lands and the annexation of formerly independent towns and cities (City of Roxbury, 1868; Dorchester, 1870; City of Charlestown, 1874; West Roxbury and Brighton, 1874) became a major expanse of land.

Four

The Back Bay

Looking toward Commonwealth Avenue from Charlesgate West in 1912, the Boylston Street Subway is being excavated. The turreted apartment building to the left of the dredger is The Hotel Charlesgate at the corner of Marlborough Street and Charlesgate East. Notice the Patrick Collins monument on the left. (Courtesy of David Rooney.)

The duplex Olney and Amory townhouses are at 413 and 415 Commonwealth Avenue. Designed by McKim, Mead and White and built in 1890, the townhouses are impressive examples of the Colonial Revival style.

William Alfred Paine (1855–1930) was a founder of Paine, Webber & Company, bankers and brokers, and lived at 409 Commonwealth Avenue, a townhouse designed by Peabody and Stearns and built in 1898.

Looking west from the Somerset Hotel, the Commonwealth Avenue Mall extends to Governor's Square (now Kenmore Square), the junction of Beacon Street and Brookline and Commonwealth Avenues. In the distance on the left is Temple Adath Israel, the Byzantine and Egyptian temple to which the congregation had moved in 1906 from the South End.

The veterans of World War I march along Commonwealth Avenue as cheering crowds wave from the windows and roofs of townhouses, line the sidewalks, and sit in temporary stands erected on the Commonwealth Avenue Mall. On the left is 24 Charlesgate East, the Minot family townhouse designed by Peabody and Stearns and built in 1891.

Looking east from Kenmore Street on the Commonwealth Avenue Mall in March 1912, townhouses line both sides of the street just before excavations were to begin for the Boylston Street Subway. (Courtesy of David Rooney.)

The townhouses on Commonwealth Avenue between Charlesgate West and Beacon Street presented an attractive streetscape of primarily Colonial Revival structures built between 1891 and 1898. On the far left are 497 and 495 Commonwealth Avenue, designed by Walker and Kimball and built in 1895; today, these two townhouses house Waterman & Sons. (Courtesy of David Rooney.)

The creation of the Fenway from the Muddy River led to the area now known as the Back Bay Fens. The classical balustrades that allow glimpses of the green space are overshadowed by the overpass that distorts the Charlesbank and this portion of the Commonwealth Avenue Mall. In the distance on the left are the apartment buildings on Massachusetts Avenue at the corner of Beacon and Marlborough Streets: the Hotel Cambridge, designed by W.T. Sears and built in 1898, and an apartment building designed by W.T. Sears and built in 1895.

A statue of Leif Eriksson, sculpted by Anne Whitney, was erected in 1887 on the edge of the Commonwealth Avenue Mall at Charlesbank East. Eriksson looks westward, obviously towards Governor's Square, now known as Kenmore Square.

The Patrick Collins Monument, sculpted by Mr. and Mrs. Henry H. Kitson, was originally located between Charlesgate East and West, adjacent to the Somerset Hotel, before it was moved to the Commonwealth Avenue Mall. Collins (1844–1905) was a "talented, honest, generous serviceable man," as the monument attests, and served not only as mayor of Boston but as a representative, senator, and consul general in London.

The Hotel Somerset was designed by Arthur Bowditch and was built in 1897 on Commonwealth Avenue at Charlesgate East. A once elegant hotel, it has since been converted to condominiums.

Muddy River was transformed by landscape architect Frederick Law Olmstead (1822–1903) into a green space that continued the Emerald Necklace that eventually encircled Boston. Extending west from the Public Garden along the Commonwealth Avenue Mall, the Charlesgate was a lush green space, and architecturally important apartment buildings, hotels, and townhouses overlooked Olmstead's creation. The Charlesgate Hotel, at the corner of Charlesgate East and Marlborough Street, was built as an elegant apartment building overlooking Olmstead's green space.

Looking west across the Muddy River (Back Bay Fens) in 1912, the townhouses in the distance face Commonwealth Avenue and are between Charlesgate West and Beacon Street. In the foreground can be seen the beginnings of the excavations for the Boylston Street Subway. (Courtesy of David Rooney.)

Work on the underground tunnel for the Boylston Street Subway was well underway in this May 1912 photograph. Looking east from about 660 Beacon Street, the Commonwealth Avenue Mall has been excavated and will become a subway station. Streetcars enter Governor's Square (now Kenmore Square) from Beacon Street on the left. On the far right can be seen the dome of the Christian Science Church. (Courtesy of David Rooney.)

Looking toward Governor's Square from Charlesgate West in 1912, this placid park will be ripped up shortly to make way for the subway excavations. The Peerless Motor Car Building (now the Boston University Bookstore) can be seen on the right, and Temple Adath Israel, built in 1906 and designed by Clarence H. Blackall, can be seen further along Commonwealth Avenue in the center of the photograph. Today, Temple Adath Israel serves as Boston University's Morse Auditorium. (Courtesy of David Rooney.)

Looking east from Brookline Avenue in 1911, Beacon Street is on the left and Commonwealth Avenue in the center of this photograph. Known originally as Governor's Square, this intersection would eventually be renamed Kenmore Square. (Courtesy of David Rooney.)

Photographed just prior to World War I, Governor's Square (now Kenmore Square) was a bustling intersection with streetcars travelling along Beacon Street and Commonwealth Avenue. Notice the entrance to the new tunnel of the Boylston Street Subway in the center of Commonwealth Avenue.

The Lindsey Mansion was designed by Chapman and Frazer and built in 1905 for William Lindsey, the inventor of an ammunition belt that was widely used during the Boer War. The mansion at 225 Bay State Road is a medieval pile of stone that was referred to as "The Castle" and is now owned by Boston University.

William Lindsey (1858–1921) was a cotton yarn salesman when his new invention, a modified ammunition belt, propelled him into a life of ease. His daughter, Leslie Lindsay, was married to Thomas Mason in the mansion in 1915 and the couple traveled to Europe on their honeymoon aboard the ill-fated *Lusitania*. The newlyweds lost their lives when the ship was torpedoed. With the sale of jewelry given to his daughter as a wedding present, Lindsey built a chapel to her memory at Emmanuel Church on Newbury Street.

The Weld Mansion was designed by Peters and Rice and built in 1900 at 149 Bay State Road for Dr. Charles Goddard Weld. A High Georgian townhouse, it was one of the last great houses to be built in the Back Bay; it now serves as offices for Boston University. On the right are 145 and 143 Bay State Road, also designed by Peters and Rice. On the left is the Pitman House, designed by Wheelwright and Haven and built in 1893.

Charles Goddard Weld (1857–1911) was a noted physician who led a comfortable life with income derived from the China trade. A well-known collector of Chinese and Japanese art, he bequeathed his magnificent collection upon his death to the Boston Museum of Fine Art.

The drawing room of the Weld Mansion at 149 Bay State Road was an impressive example of the classical style of William York Peters of the architectural firm of Peters and Rice. With classical details and silk damask wall coverings, this room was the epitome of elegance.

The library of the Weld Mansion had built-in bookcases that lined the walls and a Tudor plaster ceiling. A fireplace created just the right atmosphere for this room.

The dining room of the Weld Mansion was just off the center hall and was a mahogany-paneled room with a Tudor plaster ceiling.

The second-floor hallway of the Weld Mansion had a dramatic approach from a central staircase with a circular bronze balustrade that opened to the entrance hall below. Oak-paneled with freestanding Ionic columns, the hall connected the dining room and drawing rooms on the piano nobile.

The Maryland Apartments were designed by Charles R. Greco and built in 1925; as fewer families desired townhouses in the Back Bay after the turn of the century, apartment buildings, rather than grand townhouses, were usually built on lots of undeveloped land.

By the late 1940s, Kenmore Square was a busy intersection with buses travelling along Beacon Street and Brookline Avenue and the subway running under Commonwealth Avenue. The large apartment building at the center was designed by E.B. Stratton and built in 1923. The Kenmore Square Garage on the far left and the double-parked cars along Commonwealth Avenue on the right foreshadow today's dependency on the automobile. (Courtesy of David Rooney.)

Five
Places of Worship

Trinity Church in Copley Square is one of Boston's architectural jewels. Designed by Henry Hobson Richardson (1837–1886), a partner in the firm of Gambrill and Richardson, it was built opposite the old Museum of Fine Arts between Boylston Street and Saint James Avenue. The parish house on the left and the Hotel Westminster, the site of the John Hancock Tower by Henry Cobb of I.M. Pei & Partners, is on the right.

Arlington Street Church, the former Federal Street Church, moved to the Back Bay in 1860 when this brownstone church was completed. Designed by Arthur Gilman and Gridley J. Fox Bryant, it is a magnificent church "after the manner of Wren with a steeple such as our forefathers loved," said Charles Cummings, a well-known architect in Boston in the late nineteenth century. The church was built of New Jersey freestone and its lofty spire rises high above the trees of the Public Garden.

Looking south on Berkeley Street from Beacon Street, the First Church in Boston was built at the corner of Marlborough Street and the Central Congregational Church (now the Church of the Covenant) at Newbury Street. As their congregations moved to the new Back Bay, many of the church buildings dutifully followed their migrating flocks.

Emmanuel Church was designed by A.R. Estey and built in 1862 on Newbury Street, which was a residential street until the turn of the century. Designed as an English Gothic church and built of Roxbury puddingstone, it was the second church built in the Back Bay. A large addition was added in 1898, dwarfing the original church, and the Leslie Lindsay Chapel was built in 1920.

The Lindsay Memorial Chapel of Emmanuel Church was designed by Allen and Collens and built in 1920 as the gift of William Lindsay in memory of his daughter, Leslie Lindsay Mason, who lost her life on the *Lusitania*.

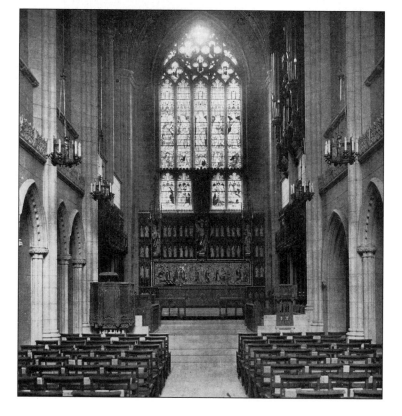

The Lindsay Memorial Chapel, designed by Allen and Collens, is a superb example of the perpendicular Gothic and is dominated by a magnificent stained-glass window and a saint-filled altar screen.

The First Church in Boston was designed by Ware and Van Brundt using Roxbury puddingstone and built in 1868 at the corner of Berkeley and Marlborough Streets. Founded in 1632, the church moved numerous times: from King (now State) Street to Washington Street, and then to Chauncey Street before finally moving to the Back Bay in 1868. The church burned in 1968 and was redesigned by Paul Rudolph in a uniquely modern approach utilizing the tower and facade that had survived the fire.

The Central Congregational Church was designed by Richard M. Upjohn and was built in 1866 at the corner of Berkeley and Newbury Streets. Built in the Gothic style of Roxbury puddingstone, it contains one of the finest collections of Tiffany glass in Boston. Today, this is the Church of the Covenant.

The Second Church in Boston was designed by Nathaniel J. Bradlee and was built in 1874 on Boylston Street between Clarendon and Dartmouth Streets in part with stones from the former church on Bedford Street. The church was to join First Church in 1912, which henceforth has been known as First and Second Church in Boston. The church was demolished in 1913 to make way for office buildings.

The Brattle Square Church was designed by H.H. Richardson and was built in 1873 at the corner of Commonwealth Avenue and Clarendon Street. After the society disbanded, the church was purchased in 1881 by the Baptists and became the First Baptist Church or the Church of the Holy Beanblowers (the latter name refers to the angel trumpeters on the corners of the Florentine tower's frieze, which represent baptism, communion, marriage, and death and were carved by Bartholdi).

The undeveloped area of Copley Square is evident in this photograph from about 1877. Trinity Church was built on 4,500 wooden piles that were driven into the marshland to support the monumental church. The Hotel Brunswick can be seen on the left and the vacant lot on the right would later be the site of the Hotel Westminster, still later the John Hancock Tower that was built in 1976.

Phillips Brooks accepted the ministry at Trinity Church and preached his first sermon on October 31, 1869. He was not just a well-respected clergyman, but he was filled with sincere compassion and possessed of the talent of expressing for every man the gospel of Jesus Christ. During his pastorate, the church on Summer Street was destroyed by the Great Boston Fire of 1872, but plans had already been underway to erect a new church in the Back Bay.

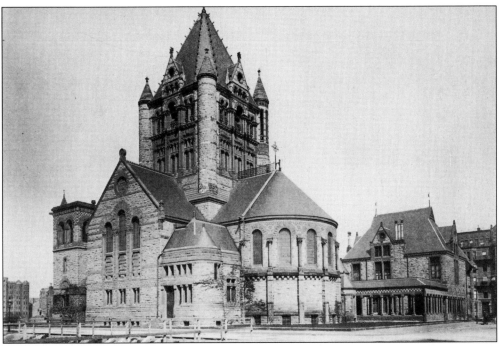

Trinity Church, seen from Clarendon Street near Saint James Avenue, was a massive granite church with Romanesque arches, patterned stone, and carved details to attest to Richardson's skill as a designer. Derived from the cathedral tower of Salamanca, the church was built between 1872 and 1877 of Dedham granite with Longmeadow freestone as well as the Westerly red granite and foundation stones from the Old Trinity Church on Summer Street. The parish house and a portion of the cloister can be seen on the right.

The Copley Square facade would evolve one further time when lanterns were added on either side of the front projection. Here, the details of Richardson's Romanesque Revival style create a straightforward and solid facade.

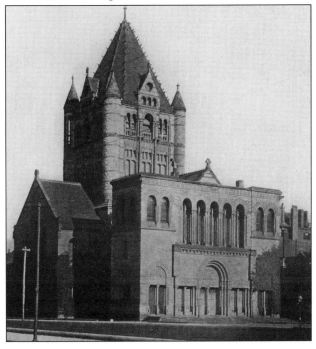

The funeral of Bishop Phillips Brooks took place on January 26, 1893, at Trinity Church. Looking from the corner of Dartmouth and Boylston Streets, the line of mourners extends from the entrance to the church for blocks.

A second funeral service was held in front of Trinity Church for the thousands of mourners who could not fit into the church. Reverend E. Winchester Donald and many other priests officiated at the funeral. In the background can be seen the Second Church in Boston and townhouses along Boylston Street.

The facade of Trinity Church was completed by the turn of the century and is still considered to be Richardson's masterpiece. The church had been built on an irregularly shaped lot, with Huntington Avenue passing at an angle. On the left can be seen the Walker and Rogers Buildings of the Massachusetts Institute of Technology and on the right the townhouses and the Hotel Westminster, the future site of the two John Hancock buildings.

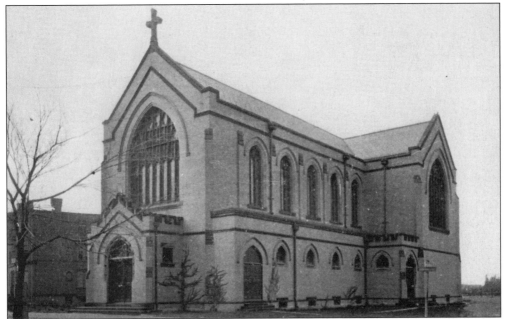

The Church of the Messiah was designed by Arthur Rotch and built in 1891 at the corner of Falmouth (now Saint Stephen's) and Gainsborough Streets. The church was designed as an early English Gothic church with yellow brick and red sandstone trim. The church later disbanded and the building was sold to the Archdiocese of Boston, who dedicated it in 1928 to Saint Ann, Mother of the Blessed Virgin.

New Old South Church was designed by Cummings and Sears as a Northern Italian Gothic church and built in 1874 at the corner of Boylston and Dartmouth Streets. The Old South Church, at the corner of Washington and Milk Streets, survived the Great Boston Fire of 1872, but the congregation had already decided to build a new church in the Back Bay. The tower had begun to lean toward the southwest and the tilt became serious enough that it had to be taken down in 1931 and rebuilt. On the right is the Boston Art Club, designed by William Ralph Emerson and built in 1881.

The Hollis Street Church was designed by George Meacham and was built in 1884 at the corner of Exeter and Newbury Streets. The church, a brick Byzantine structure with a peculiar tower, was later used as the Copley Methodist Episcopal Church and was demolished in 1966.

Edward Everett Hale (1822–1909) was the pastor of the Hollis Street Church, or the South Congregational Church in Boston. A noted preacher, he served as chaplain of the United States Senate and was the author of *A Man Without A Country*. On the base of Hale's statue in the Public Garden, sculpted by Bela L. Pratt and unveiled in 1913, is the following inscription: "Man of Letters—Preacher of the Gospel—Prophet of Peace—Patriot."

Saint Cecelia's Church was dedicated in 1888 and is on Belvidere Street between Massachusetts Avenue and Dalton Street.

Saint Clement's was built as a Universalist church and is one of the finest examples of the English Gothic in Boston. Built at the corner of Boylston and Ipswich Streets, it was purchased by the Archdiocese of Boston and dedicated by Cardinal O'Connell in 1935. In 1945, then Archbishop, later Cardinal, Cushing designated Saint Clement's as the Archdiocesan Eucharistic Shrine.

The Romanesque Revival Church of Christ, Scientist was designed by Franklin I. Welch and built in 1895 and was the first church built by founder Mary Baker Eddy in Boston. The church still survives at the former corner of Falmouth and Norway Streets, now part of the Christian Science Mall.

"Mother's Room" was the private parlor-office of Mary Baker Eddy and was a comfortably furnished room with stained-glass windows. On a tablet under the windows is engraved the following: "A Testimonial to our Beloved Teacher, the Reverend Mary Baker Eddy, Discoverer and Founder of Christian Science, Author of its Textbook, "Science and Health, with Key to the Scriptures;" President of the Massachusetts Metaphysical College, and the First Pastor of this Denomination."

The First Church of Christ, Scientist was designed by Charles Brigham and built in 1906 facing Huntington Avenue between Falmouth, Norway, and Saint Paul Streets. Ieoh Ming Pei of I.M. Pei and Partners added a colonnade in the late 1970s to complete an aspect of Brigham's design that was never built. On the right is the old church built in 1895.

The Christian Science complex had grown to include a major section of land bounded by Huntington and Massachusetts Avenues and Saint Botolph Street. The lush green lawns were dotted with shaped trees and have offered respite during summer months, never more so than after the reflecting pool was constructed in the late 1970s.

Six

Institutions, Colleges, and Schools

The city block bounded by Berkeley, Boylston, Clarendon, and Newbury Streets was the site of the Boston Society of Natural History and the Rogers and Walker Buildings of the Massachusetts Institute of Technology. Two carriages pass in front of the natural history museum, which was designed by William Gibbons Preston and built of brick and freestone in 1863. Formerly Bonwit Teller's, today it is Louis of Boston.

The museum of the Boston Society of Natural History was designed by William Gibbons Preston and built in 1863 at the corner of Berkeley and Boylston Streets. Notice the vast expanse of undeveloped land in the new Back Bay; on the left can be seen the laying of the foundations for the Rogers Building of the Massachusetts Institute of Technology and on the right the townhouses on Beacon Street between Berkeley and Clarendon Streets.

The Museum of Natural History was to move to the Charles River Dam in 1947, where it reopened as the Boston Museum of Science. The old museum building was remodeled as Bonwit Teller's and more recently as Louis of Boston.

The stretch of Boylston Street between Berkeley and Clarendon Streets contained three impressive buildings. From the right are the Museum of Natural History and the Rogers and Walker Buildings of the Massachusetts Institute of Technology.

William Barton Rogers (1804–1882) was the founder and first president of the Massachusetts Institute of Technology, and the first president of the American Association for the Advancement of Science.

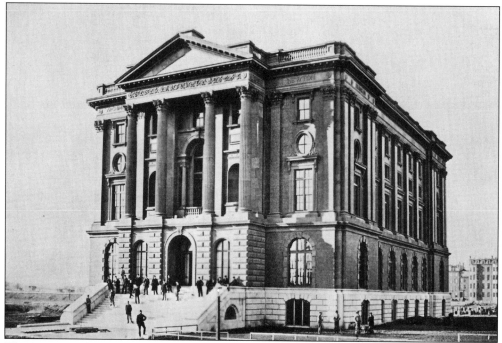

The Rogers Building was an impressive French Academic building that was completed in 1865. Designed by William Gibbons Preston, it was the site of the first architectural school in the United States (established by William R. Ware) and the location of the first Lowell Lectures. The building was demolished in 1939, and the New England Mutual Life Insurance Company built its headquarters on the site. The latter building was designed by Cram and Ferguson, and further enlarged in 1963 by Hoyle, Doran and Berry.

The Chemical Labratory Classes at Their Studies at the Massachusetts Institute of Technology was drawn by A. Bergham and was published in *Leslie's Illustrated Newspaper* on December 18, 1869. Interestingly, the first female student at MIT was Ellen Swallow Richards, who entered as an "experimental student" and went on to spend her career in educating the public on nutrition. (Courtesy of Virginia M. White.)

Students in the life class at MIT (often referred to as "Tech") draw a male model, who poses on the right. As many of the students went on to study architecture, these drawing classes were not only fun but worthwhile.

After the Massachusetts Institute of Technology moved in 1913 across the Charles River to a new campus in Cambridge, the Rogers Building was often used for classes in landscaping and horticulture. Unfortunately, this elegant building was demolished in 1939 to make way for an insurance company.

The Walker Building of the Massachusetts Institute of Technology was designed by Carl Fehmer and built in 1883 at the corner of Boylston and Clarendon Streets. The Walker Building was named for Dr. W.J. Walker of Newport, Rhode Island, a generous benefactor of MIT in the nineteenth century.

The Laboratory of Electrical Engineering at MIT was located in the Walker Building. Here two students study the efficiency of ventilating fans by an electrical method.

In the Laboratory of Applied Mechanics at MIT, students test the efficiency of screw jacks.

Many of the students at MIT went on to become architects and engineers, and experiments such as those conducted with the masonary arch testing machine led to a better understanding of stress and load on an arch. A student stands beside the machine in 1908.

The Harvard Medical School was designed by Ware and Van Brunt and built in 1881 at the corner of Boylston and Exeter Streets, next to the future site of the Boston Public Library. After the medical school relocated to Longwood Avenue in the Fenway, the building was used by Boston University for its College of Liberal Arts.

Members of the life class at the Cowles Art School pose for their class portrait in 1895. Founded by Frank M. Cowles in 1883, the Cowles Art School was at 145 Dartmouth Street with "a staff of 9 instructors, and an attendance of about 240."

Mechanic Arts High School was on Dalton Street in the Back Bay. In the distance on the far right can be seen the Romanesque Revival fire station at the corner of Boylston and Hereford Streets. (Courtesy of David Rooney.)

Students in a "smithy" class learn the trade of a smith, or a blacksmith, who makes or repairs metal objects. A century ago, smiths not only made horseshoes but provided a necessary repair service for the public.

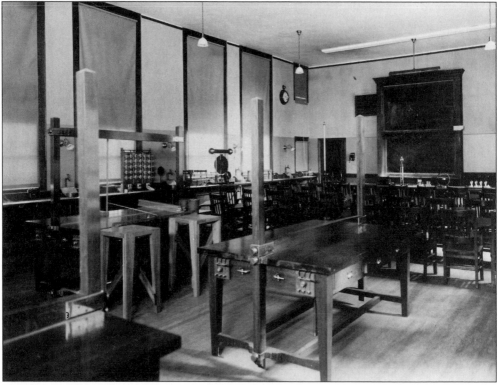

The physical laboratory at Mechanic Arts High School was photographed about 1908. The clock was manufactured by the Blodgett Clock Company. (Courtesy of David Rooney.)

A class at the Mechanic Arts High School studies in a large classroom in June of 1899. (Courtesy of David Rooney.)

The Prince School was designed by city architect George A. Clough and was built in 1881 at the corner of Newbury and Exeter Streets. The school was named for Frederick O. Prince, a mayor of Boston. The former school building was converted into luxury condominiums with ground-floor shops in 1982. (Courtesy of David Rooney.)

Frederick Octavius Prince (1818–1899) was mayor of Boston in 1877 and again from 1879 to 1881. As mayor, he improved the East Boston ferries, adopted the public park scheme, improved the city's sewerage system, and was instrumental in erecting the English and Latin High School Buildings on Warren Avenue in the South End.

The drawing room of the Commonwealth Avenue School was an elegant room in a home and day school established by the Misses Hannah and Julia Gilman.

The drawing room in Miss Frances V. Emerson's home and Day School for Girls was an elegantly appointed room with copious books, artwork, and enlightening bibelots. Miss Emerson's school was at 18 Newbury Street.

Seven

Art Square or Copley Square

Copley Square is the junction of Boylston, Dartmouth and Blagdon Streets and Huntington and Saint James Avenues. Originally known as Art Square, as the original Museum of Fine Arts faced the square, it was renamed Copley Square on February 21, 1883, in honor of John Singleton Copley, a noted painter who once lived on Beacon Hill. Today, the McKim Building of the Boston Public Library (on the right) dominates the square. In this photograph of 1905, the Museum of Fine Arts can be seen on the left and the S.S. Pierce & Company store, designed by Edwin S. Tobey, is in the center.

The coliseum in which the Peace Jubilee of 1869 was held was a mammoth structure that was built by Judah Sears & Son on the site of the present Back Bay railroad station. Following the Civil War, the Peace Jubilee was held to celebrate "in festive fashion peace and the gathering of the Southern States back into the fold." The festival organizer, Patrick S. Gilmore, directed a chorus of ten thousand voices with an orchestra of a thousand instruments!

Patrick Sarsfield Gilmore was the organizer and director of the Peace Jubilee and International Music Festival. He conducted the "Anvil Chorus," into which one hundred red-shirted firemen were drafted to bring out the staccato parts by hammering on individual anvils. Gilmore's conducting of the Anvil Chorus was so moving that observers heard "hands clap, feet stamp and canes pound the floor."

The original Museum of Fine Arts was designed by Sturgis and Brigham and was opened to the public on July 4, 1876. A Ruskinian Gothic building that "underwent considerable adverse criticism at the time of its erection," it was on Saint James Street between Trinity Place and Dartmouth Street, the present site of the Copley Plaza Hotel. The rich details of the museum's facade included tablets depicting the "Genius of Art" and "Art and Industry" on either end of the building.

A woman sketches one of the plaster bas reliefs that adorned the Museum of Fine Arts in the late nineteenth century. In the first decades after its opening in 1876, the museum purchased plaster castings of classical sculptures and statues as it was deemed a prudent expenditure considering the expense of original pieces of art. At one time, by 1890, there were nearly a thousand plaster castings displayed in galleries on the first floor of the museum.

The Museum of Fine Arts was an impressive Ruskinian Gothic building by Sturgis and Brigham with lancet windows and a plethora of English terra cotta ornamentation. After its completion in 1876, the building was doubled in size with a flanking wing built on the east side, or the left of this photograph. Dartmouth Street, seen on the right, led to the Back Bay Depot and the South End.

A gallery of the Museum of Fine Arts had many of the paintings that still grace the galleries of the present museum. Art students pose on the right, resting from their labors of copying the original paintings.

Prince Henry of Prussia, brother of Kaiser Wilhelm, visited Boston in 1902. He sits in a carriage in the center of Copley Square with numerous well-wishers gathered for his arrival. In the background are Trinity Church, the Hotel Westminster, and the old Museum of Fine Arts.

Samuel Brown built his townhouse on Dartmouth Street at the corner of Blagden Street. A fashionable French Academic townhouse with a mansard roof, it was demolished in 1888 to make way for the McKim Building of the Boston Public Library. On the right can be seen the unfinished tower of the New Old South Church on Boylston Street.

Trinity Church dominates the east side of Copley Square with its parish house on the left. On the right can be seen the old Museum of Fine Arts and the Hotel Westminster to its left, now the site of the John Hancock Tower. The Westminster had elaborate terra cotta decorations and caryatids sculpted by Max Bachman.

This dramatic statue of Phillips Brooks (1835–1893) was sculpted by Augustus Saint Gaudens and was placed in a baldachino designed by McKim, Mead and White near the north wall of Trinity Church. A rector of Trinity Church, Brooks was later to become bishop of Boston.

The south wall of the Boston Public Library at the corner of Dartmouth and Blagden Streets was erected block by block until the facility was completed in 1895 and opened as the "Palace of the People."

The facade of McKim's Boston Public Library is one of the city's most impressive designs, imparting a sense of dignity and stateliness to Copley Square. Built to emulate an Italian palazzo, on either side of the Dartmouth Street entrance are two sculptures by Bela L. Pratt (1867–1917). These colossal seated sculptures, *Science* and *Art*, add to the magnificence of this Renaissance inspired library, as do the fantastic lanterns.

The memorial lions that flank the grand staircase in the Boston Public Library were sculpted by Louis Saint Gaudens. The grand staircase is of yellow Siena marble and there are wall murals by Puvis de Chauvannes.

The Muses Welcoming the Genius of Enlightenment was a wall mural by Puvis de Chauvannes at the Boston Public Library. The inside also has frescos and murals by Edwin Austin Abbey and John Singer Sargent, making the interior as impressive as the exterior.

Bates Hall, named for patron and benefactor Joshua L. Bates, is a grand reading room that is 218 feet in length and has a barrel-vaulted ceiling and massive arched windows that overlook Copley Square.

The magazine room in the Boston Public Library was a two-story affair that seemed to contain every magazine imaginable. A vaulted ceiling of yellow brick was supported by Doric columns, and art and sculpture was placed so as to please the readers.

The courtyard of the Boston Public Library is still an oasis from the city. Wooden benches line the arched passages and open onto a pleasure garden.

Bacchante and Child was sculpted by Frederick Mac Monnies (1865–1937) and was placed in the center of the courtyard. The gift of William F. McKim, its graceful, nude, dancing figure with grapes being offered to the child caused such an uproar that the statue was withdrawn and donated by McKim to the Metropolitan Museum of Art in New York. A copy was ordered by George R. White, who donated it to the Boston Museum of Fine Arts, where it still graces the garden courtyard on Huntington Avenue.

A streetcar heads east on Boylston Street about 1905. The Boston Public Library and the Harvard Medical School are visible behind it.

The western flank of Copley Square contained the Boston Public Library in the center, the New Old South Church, and the Second Church in Boston.

Boylston Street is being excavated for the Boylston Street Subway in this photograph of 1913. Trinity Church dominates the square, and the spires of the Central Congregational Church (now the Church of the Covenant) and Arlington Street Church can be seen to the left. Notice the staging that has been erected to construct new office buildings on Boylston Street between Clarendon and Dartmouth Streets. (Courtesy of David Rooney.)

Boylston Street at the corner of Dartmouth Street had evolved from a residential area with the Chauncey Hall School and the Second Church in Boston to a business district, as seen in this photograph of 1911. The townhouse on the corner was built in 1879 by Samuel Carlton and had become a storefront three decades later. The Second Church, built in 1873 by Nathaniel J. Bradlee, was to be demolished in 1913.

Taking part in a parade of Boston suffragettes in 1914 were, from the left, Helen Keller, her secretary Pauline Thompson, and her teacher, Mrs. J.A. Macy. In the background is the facade of Trinity Church in Copley Square.

In November of 1911, the new Copley Plaza Hotel was being erected on Saint James Street, the former site of the Museum of Fine Arts. Designed by Henry Hardenbergh, architect of The Plaza (now Trump Plaza) in New York, the Copley Plaza was opened in 1912 and is considered Boston's grand dame of hotels. Trinity Church and the Hotel Westminster are to the left of the hotel. (Courtesy of David Rooney.)

Looking down Saint James Avenue from Dartmouth Street and Huntington Avenue in 1913, a streetcar heads west as it passes in front of Trinity Church. (Courtesy of David Rooney.)

Looking west on Saint James Street in 1913, the entrance to the Hotel Westminster can be seen on the left and the Copley Plaza just beyond. The Boston Public Library was built between 1887 and 1895 on the Dartmouth Street block between Blagden (on the left) and Boylston Streets. (Courtesy of David Rooney.)

Eight
Elegant Hotels

The Commonwealth Avenue Mall stretches from Arlington Street at the Public Garden to the Muddy River, today's Fenway. Though developed as a residential neighborhood, the Back Bay was to include both residential and transient hotels, among them the Hotel Vendome, seen here in a photograph of 1895. The Back Bay also included numerous churches; from the left are the spires of the Brattle Square Church (now the First Baptist Church), the Central Congregational Church (now the Church of the Covenant), the Arlington Street Church, and Trinity Church, and the dome of the New Old South Church.

William Gibbons Preston (1842–1910) designed the Hotel Vendome in the French Academic style with both Italian and Tuckahoe marble for the exterior. The hotel, built in 1871 at the corner of Dartmouth Street and Commonwealth Avenue, was just two blocks north of Copley Square and it faced the Commonwealth Avenue Mall. The townhouses to the right would be demolished when the hotel was enlarged by J.F. Ober in 1881.

A guest with his leather suitcase and a doorman flank a gas street lamp in front of the Dartmouth Street entrance to the Hotel Vendome about 1900. As a "transient hotel," a place where one stayed for a short period of time rather than an apartment hotel, the Vendome was considered the epitome of elegance and comfort. Today, after a disastrous fire in 1972, the Vendome has been developed as inexpensive condominiums. (Courtesy of David Rooney.)

The Hotel Vendome was such a success that an addition by J.F. Ober was built along Commonwealth Avenue in 1881, dwarfing the original hotel on the left. The first commercial use of incandescent lamps in New England took place here in 1882. After a disastrous fire in 1972, the hotel was redesigned as inexpensive condominiums, and provided commercial space in the heart of the Back Bay on the first floor.

The Hotel Brunswick was designed by Sturgis and Brigham and built in 1873 at the corner of Boylston and Clarendon Streets, with an annex being added four years later. Notice the wood railings surrounding the undeveloped lot in the foreground, the future site of the Hotel Bristol (L. Newcomb, 1879) and the Hotel Cluny (J.P. Putnam, 1876).

By the turn of the century, the Hotel Brunswick was considered to be among the most fashionable hotels in Boston. A streetcar heads west on Boylston Street and a hackney carriage waits for passengers on the Clarendon Street side of the hotel.

The office and rotunda of the Hotel Brunswick were contained in an elegantly decorated space with a grand staircase that descended to a marble-floored lobby.

One of the features of the Hotel Brunswick was its Venetian Room, which contained a chandelier of Morano glass and "Italian" decor that included richly upholstered furniture and a frieze of Iris. The lavish use of furniture and objects d'art made these hotels the epitome of fashion and comfort.

The Hotel Victoria was a brick apartment hotel designed by J.L. Faxon and built in 1886 with a distinctly Moorish feel. There was a crenellated roof cornice at the corner of Dartmouth and Newbury Streets. The hotel was considered to have had a quiet, refined, and homelike atmosphere and was one block north of Copley Square.

Copley-Plaza Hotel, Boston, Mass.

The Copley Plaza Hotel was opened in 1912 on the site of the first Boston Museum of Fine Arts. Designed by Henry Hardenburg, architect of The Plaza in New York City, it is a marble and limestone hotel that faces Copley Square. The Copley Plaza is celebrating its 75th anniversary this year.

John Fitzgerald, a former mayor of Boston known as "Honey Fitz," and his friend Sir Thomas Lipton pose in front of the entrance to the Copley Plaza Hotel in 1923.

Saint James Street was a busy thoroughfare in 1913, with streetcars passing every few minutes destined for all parts of the city. On the left is the corner of Trinity Church, with the Hotel Westminster next to the Copley Plaza. The Hotel Westminster was demolished when the John Hancock Tower was built.

Though the gilded lions flanking the entrance to the Copley Plaza Hotel seem to have been there since the hotel was built, they were originally in front of the Hotel Kensington on Boylston Street, as seen on the left. In this 1912 photograph, street workers are preparing for the Boylston Street Subway as a streetcar heads west toward the Fenway. The spire of the New Old South Church looms on the left and the McKim Building of the Boston Public Library is on the right. (Courtesy of David Rooney.)

The Hotel Lenox was designed by Arthur H. Bowditch and built in 1901 at the corner of Boylston and Exeter Streets. The excavations for the Boylston Street Subway in 1912 can be seen on the right and pedestrians walk along Boylston Street on the left. (Courtesy of David Rooney.)

The Exeter Street entrance to the Hotel Lenox, photographed in 1937, is a rusticated base of limestone with brick and terra cotta above. An addition and renovations to the hotel were made by Clarence Blackall of Blackall and Clapp. (Courtesy of David Rooney.)

The Italian Room in the Hotel Lenox was designed by Carroll Bill and the furniture was made by Irving & Casson, A.H. Davenport Company of Boston. The stenciled, beamed ceiling, leather-upholstered chairs, and tapestries lent a somewhat ambiguous atmosphere to the room.

The Statler Hotel was to be built at the corner of Saint James and Arlington Streets. This area of the Back Bay remained open into the twentieth century, though it was only one block south of Boylston Street. A sign on the upper left announces that this lot will be the future site of Paine's Furniture Company. On the immediate left is the future site of the Statler Hotel (now the Park Plaza) and Office Building, designed by George B. Post and built in 1925. (Courtesy of David Rooney.)

The skeletal frame of the Ritz Carlton Hotel was photographed in 1926 as it rose at the corner of Arlington and Newbury Streets. The uniformity of the rooflines in the Back Bay had, in most cases, been maintained until Haddon Hall (designed by J.P. Putnam and built in 1894) and the Hotel Westminster broke the height restrictions. The Ritz Carlton Hotel would be a high-rise hotel with a rooftop garden overlooking the Public Garden. (Courtesy of David Rooney.)

A uniformed doorman stands in front of the Arlington Street entrance to the new Ritz Carlton Hotel, which opened on May 18, 1927. The use of limestone with exaggerated neoclassical details—such as the arches surmounting the windows of the dining room—made for an impressive facade that faced the Public Garden.

Designed by the architectural firm of Strickland, Blodgett & Law, the Ritz Carlton Hotel has been the epitome of style and elegance since 1927. Two men converse in the Public Garden and the spire of the Central Congregational Church (now Church of the Covenant) rises on Newbury Street.

The lounge of the Ritz Carlton Hotel is on the first floor, on the right as one enters from Arlington Street. Comfortably furnished, it might be considered a private drawing room if this were not a hotel. Woodward Wyner, owner of the Ritz Carlton, never compromised on service, making the hotel one of the best run in the world.

The barbershop was one of the added luxuries made available to guests at the Ritz Carlton Hotel. Sheathed in pine paneling, it was a distinctly masculine room where one could get a trim or a shave.

In the 1920s and after, Newbury Street began to lose its residential aspect when many of the townhouses were converted to shops catering to the carriage trade and educational institutions. In some cases, the facades were rebuilt with exaggerated Neoclassical details; others were demolished and new buildings built. The building at 93 Newbury had a new storefront designed by J.R. Ward built in 1925. On the left is Edward F. Kakas & Sons, a well-known furrier that moved to Roxbury this year.

As the Back Bay continued to attract bon ton shops, many people would drive to town for shopping. Here a parking lot in Park Square, located directly behind Paine's Furniture Company and utilized by shoppers and workers alike, became a sea of cars in the late 1920s. Today, parking is still one of the major concerns for those whose destination is the Back Bay of Boston! (Courtesy of David Rooney.)

Acknowledgments

I would like to thank the following individuals and institutions for their assistance in researching this book on Boston's Back Bay. In many instances, their generosity in the loaning of photographs, stereoscopic views, and books on the history and development of the Back Bay has been of tremendous help, and I appreciate their continued interest in and support of the Images of America series:

Betsey Adams, Daniel J. Ahlin, Rosamond Warren Allen, Susan Ashbrook, Jamie Brennan, Paul and Helen Graham Buchanan, John Burrows, Jamie Carter (my patient editor), Janice Chadbourne (fine arts department of the Boston Public Library), Frank Cheney, Elizabeth Williams Clapp, Edith G. Clifford, Lorna Condon (Society for the Preservation of New England Antiquities), Dexter, William Dillon, Sheila Donahue, the Doric Dames of the Massachusetts State House, John Fox, the late Walter S. Fox, the late Rosamond Gifford, Edward W. Gordon (executive director of The Gibson House), Jack Grinold, Richard Griswold, Helen Hannon, Lecia Harbison, Pauline Chase Harrell, David Hessey, David Hocker, Elizabeth Bradford Hough, James Z. Kyprianos, Mary Leen, Jonathan T. Melick, Maureen Meister (president of The Gibson Society), Phyllis Meyer, John Norton, Stephen and Susan Paine, Reverend Michael Parise, William H. Pear, Sally Pierce (The Boston Athenaeum), David Rooney, Dennis Ryan, Anthony and Mary Mitchell Sammarco, the late Charlotte Tuttle Clapp Sammarco, Rosemary Sammarco, Sylvia Sandeen, Robert Bayard Severy, Catherina Slautterback (The Boston Athenaeum), Jon Stephenson, Esq., Joyce Stevens (Heritage Education), Wendy Swanton, Catherine Seiberling Pond, Laurie Thomas, William Varrell, Dorothy C. Wallace, and Marion Woodbridge.

A portion of the royalties from this book will benefit The Gibson House Museum. Built in 1860 at 137 Beacon Street by the Gibson Family, and designed by the noted architect Edward Clarke Cabot, it is the historic house of Boston's Back Bay.